SHELL SCRIPTING

Learn Linux Shell Programming Step-By-Step

Harry Harvey

TABLE OF CONTENT

Chapter 1

Introduction to Shell Scripting

What you will learn in this chapter

Φ Introduction to UNIX and Linux operating systems

Φ Understanding Shell Scripting

What you will need for this chapter

Φ PC with Linux / UNIX operating system

What is the UNIX/Linux?

UNIX is one of the most popular operating systems that originally was developed by Bell labs in 1970s. UNIX also is multiuser computer operating system that means many users can open and use the shell to access the kernel at the same time. UNIX is a commercial operating system.

Linux is an operating system like UNIX operating system but it's an open source and open source here means that you can take a look at the internal design (Kernel) and its code also you can modify and customize it, Linux operating system can be used on servers, PCs, mobile devices and embedded devices or non –computer devices. There are many distributions   or versions of Linux such as Ubuntu, Debian, Kubunt, Red hat, Fedora, OpenSUSE and many more.

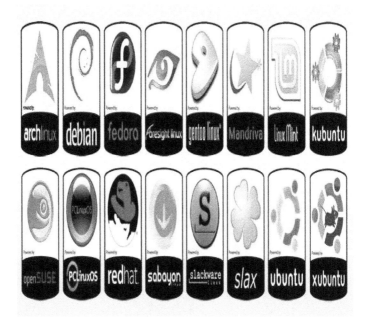

Understanding the Shell

I know that you have a question which is "what is the shell exactly?" the shell is the command line that you use to access the kernel of the operating system , to make it clear the shell is simply a program that takes your commands from your keyboard and passes them to the operating system. All Linux versions support the shell program from the GNU project called Bash. The name Bash stands for "Bourne Again Shell", the original UNIX shell developed by Steve Bourne.

If you look at your desktop menus, you can find one of the shells. The GNOME desktop environment uses gnome – terminal and KDE uses Konsole, you can simply call it "terminal" on your menu. There are a lot of terminal emulators that available for Linux operating system, but you can use anyone for the same purpose because they do the same thing; which allows you to access to the shell, so let's start to work with the emulator , you will see something like that [YourUser @ linux ~] $

This is called the shell prompt and will see it if the shell is ready to receive your input, also you may see it in another look depending on the distribution you use, the line above means the following YourUser = username, linux = machinename and it will be followed with your current working space. You may see "#" or "$" at the end of the prompt

● "#" → this means you have the super user privileges

● "$" → this means you don't have the administrator privileges

Let's enter any random command at the prompt

[Youruser @ linux ~] $ dfdf454df

The shell will tell the following

Bash: dfdf454df: command not found

[Youruser @ linux ~] $

The history of your command

If you want to repeat any command without writing it again you can just press the up arrow button on your keyboard

● keep in mind that ctrl + c and ctrl + v to copy and paste don't work on the shell

Let's write some commands

[Youruser @ linux ~] $ date

Sat Jul 29 17:39:28 EET 2017

Form its name the date can be uses to show the current date

[Youruser @ linux ~] $ cal

July 2017

Su Mo Tu We Th Fr Sa

1

2 3 4 5 6 7 8

9 10 11 12 13 14 15

16 17 18 19 20 21 22

23 24 25 26 27 28 29

30 31

The cal command is a related command to the date command which can be used to show you the calendar

If you would like to see the details of your free space you can write df

c

Filesystem	1K-blocks	Used	Available	Use%	Mounted on
/dev/sda1	19620732	4600964	14000020	25%	/
udev	10240	0	10240	0%	/dev
tmpfs	217280	5104	212176	3%	/run
tmpfs	543196	160	543036	1%	/dev/shm
tmpfs	5120	4	5116	1%	/run/lock
tmpfs	543196	0	543196	0%	/sys/fs/cgroup

Also you can write the free command to take a look at the free space of the memory

[Youruser @ linux ~] $ free

total	used	free	shared	buffers	cached
Mem:	1086392	1007544	78848	3036	53092
295252					
-/+ buffers/cache:	659200	427192			
Swap:	901116	12888	888228		

If you would like to end the terminal session or close it you can use the **exit** command

[Youruser @ linux ~] $ exit

Navigation

If you would like to be clever in working with the shell you should know how to navigate the file system on Linux. There are three important commands

- cd → change directory

- pwd → this command can be used to print the current working directory

- ls → this command you will use to list the content of the current directory

In Linux the first directory is called root, you should be aware that the directories in Linux organized in a tree pattern (directory in Linux like folder in windows), in windows there is a separate file system for every device / storage but in Linux/UNIX there is a single file system tree

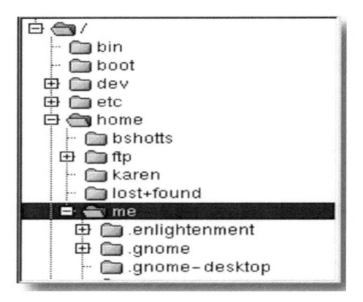

If you would like to show the current work directory write the pwd command on the terminal

[Youruser @ linux ~] $ pwd

/home/me

● **In Linux every user has its own home directory**

Now let's show the contents of the directory, just write the command ls on your terminal window

[Youruser @ linux ~] $ ls

Desktop Documents Music   Public

Desktop Downloads Pictures Templates Videos

The third important command is the cd command

To change the working directory, you can write the command cd followed by the pathname

[Youruser @ linux ~] $ cd /usr/bin

[Youruser @ linux ~] $ pwd

/usr/bin

[Youruser @ linux bin] $ ls

[**pamoil**

2to3   **pamon**

2to3-2.7   **pamstack**

13

2to3-3.4	pamstretch
411toppm	pamstretch-gen
7z	paperconf
7za	paplay
a2p	parec
aconnect	parecord
acpi	parsechangelog
acpi_listen	partx
addpart	passwd
alacarte	paste
alsaloop	pasuspender

Questions

1. What is the Linux?

2. What are the funcitons of the shell

3. Which command can be used for the following

   - Change directory

   - Print the current working directory

   - Show the free space of the memory

Chapter 2

Explore your system

What you will learn in this chapter

Φ Understanding the file, less, ls commands

Φ Know the important directories of any Linux distro

What you will need for this chapter

Φ PC with Linux / UNIX operating system

Enjoy working with the command line

Let's try to move around your file system, this time will be to go deeper with your Linux file system, so you will learn more commands for this purpose

- ls – you can use this command to list directory contents

- file – this command can be used to determine the file type

- less – you will use the less command to view the contents

You can start writing with ls command

[Youruser @ linux ~] $ ls

Desktop Games Audio Photos Public Templates Videos

Also you can specify the directory that you want to show what its contents

[Youruser @ linux ~] $ ls /usr

bin games include lib local sbin share src x86_64-linux-gnu

You can also use this command to show more details

[Youruser @ linux ~] $ ls -l

total 56

drwxr-xr-x 2 Youruser 4096 Jun 13 15:33 Desktop

drwxr-xr-x 2 Youruser 4096 Apr 22 12:32 Documents

drwxr-xr-x 2 Youruser 4096 Apr 22 12:32 Downloads

-rw-r--r-- 1 Youruser 8980 Apr 22 12:02 examples.desktop

-rw-rw-r-- 1 Youruser 1050 Apr 27 09:36 Hello.cpp

-rw-rw-r-- 1 Youruser 139 Apr 27 09:36 Hello.layout

drwxr-xr-x 2 Youruser 4096 Apr 22 12:32 Music

drwxr-xr-x 2 Youruser 4096 Apr 22 12:32 Pictures

drwxr-xr-x 2 Youruser 4096 Apr 22 12:32 Public

drwxrwxr-x 3 Youruser 4096 Apr 27 10:32 sketchbook

drwxr-xr-x 2 Youruser 4096 Apr 22 12:32 Templates

drwxr-xr-x 2 Youruser 4096 Apr 22 12:32 Videos

After adding the l you actually changed the format of the output

Options and arguments

When you want to write a command you mostly will follow the command with an option or an argument (one or more). So the command will look like the following

command -option argument

[Youruser @ linux ~] $ ls -l

[Youruser @ linux ~] $ ls -l –reverse

For example the ls command has a lot of options

-a | –all | to list all files

-A | --almost-all | to list all the files but without listing the current and the parent directory

-d | --directory | if you specified a directory in this case the ls will show the content of this directory

-F | --classify | to append the character at the end of your listed name

-h | --human-readable | to display the size of the files in a readable language

And many more…

If you would like to know the type of any file you can use the command file followed by the filename, for example:

[Youruser @ linux ~] $ cd /usr/bin

[Youruser@linux:/usr/bin]$ ls

[	mcd
2to3	mcheck
2to3-2.7	mclasserase
2to3-3.4	mcomp
a2p	mcookie
aconnect	mcopy
acpi_listen	mc-tool
activity-log-manager	mc-wait-for-name
add-apt-repository	md5sum
addpart	md5sum.textutils
addr2line	mdel

alsaloop   mdeltree

you will see something like that (and more files)

[Youruser@linux:/usr/bin]$ file mcd

mcd: symbolic link to `mtools'

Let's show the file content with the less command

less is a command to show you the content of a file

you can write it as the following less + your filename

for example

[Youruser @ linux ~] $ cd /usr/bin

[Youruser@linux:/usr/bin]$ ls

Youruser@linux:/usr/bin]$ less /etc/passwd

root:x:0:0:root:/root:/bin/bash

daemon:x:1:1:daemon:/usr/sbin:/usr/sbin/nologin

bin:x:2:2:bin:/bin:/usr/sbin/nologin

sys:x:3:3:sys:/dev:/usr/sbin/nologin

sync:x:4:65534:sync:/bin:/bin/sync

games:x:5:60:games:/usr/games:/usr/sbin/nologin

man:x:6:12:man:/var/cache/man:/usr/sbin/nologin

lp:x:7:7:lp:/var/spool/lpd:/usr/sbin/nologin

mail:x:8:8:mail:/var/mail:/usr/sbin/nologin

news:x:9:9:news:/var/spool/news:/usr/sbin/nologin

uucp:x:10:10:uucp:/var/spool/uucp:/usr/sbin/nologin

proxy:x:13:13:proxy:/bin:/usr/sbin/nologin

www-data:x:33:33:www-data:/var/www:/usr/sbin/nologin

backup:x:34:34:backup:/var/backups:/usr/sbin/nologin

list:x:38:38:Mailing List Manager:/var/list:/usr/sbin/nologin

You will get something like that you can press space to reach to the end

kernoops:x:112:65534:Kernel Oops Tracking Daemon,,,:/:/bin/false

pulse:x:113:124:PulseAudio daemon,,,:/var/run/pulse:/bin/false

rtkit:x:114:126:RealtimeKit,,,:/proc:/bin/false

saned:x:115:127::/var/lib/saned:/bin/false

usbmux:x:116:46:usbmux daemon,,,:/var/lib/usbmux:/bin/false

colord:x:117:128:colord colour management daemon,,,:/var/lib/colord:/bin/false

hplip:x:118:7:HPLIP system user,,,:/var/run/hplip:/bin/false

lightdm:x:119:129:Light Display Manager:/var/lib/lightdm:/bin/false

youruser:x:1000:1000:BebO,,,:/home/bebo:/bin/bash

(END)

Less commands / options

q → exit less

b → back one page

h → to display the help screen

g → go to the end of the file

Important Directories on any Linux system

/ → the root directory or the start point that everything start from

/bin→ in this directory you can find the booting file system

/dev→ this directory has the device nodes (contain the system device as files)

/etc→ this directory has the system config files and scripts for the system services

/home→ home is the directory that every user account can write in

/usr/bin → has the entire installed programs for linux distro/version

/usr/local → has the programs that you have installed

/var→ this directory tree you can use it to change your data (DBs, Mails)

/proc → it's a virtual file system to show you how the kernel organize your computer

Questions

1. If you want to list the content of any directory, what command you will use?

2. Define the usage of the following

   - /

   - /root

   - /usr/b

3. What is the difference between the less and the ls commands?

Chapter 3

Change and Manipulate your files

What you will learn in this chapter

Φ Create and manipulate files

Φ What you will need for this chapter

Φ PC with Linux / UNIX operating system

Manipulate your directories

In this part you will work with the following commands

• **cp** → you will use this command to copy files and directories

• **mv** → to move or rename your files and directories

• **rm** → to delete your files or directories

• **mkdir** → to create a directory

• **ln** → to create hard links

You can use these command to manipulate either your files or directories on Linux

27

Actually, I know that you have now a question in your mind which is "why we use these commands to copy, paste, cut, delete files although we can use the file manager instead of the command line?"

The answer is so easy: the command line is more powerful and more flexible

For have example, if you a lot of files that should be manipulated, in this case if you use the command line it will be much easier than using the file manager

What is wildcards or globbing?

Wildcard or globbing is a feature in shell that allows you to select the files based on patterns of characters

Examples of wildcards

    * →To match your characters

    ?→ For matching single characters

    [Characters] →you can match a character that is one of the group of characters

[! Characters] →you can match a character that is not one of the group of characters

[[: class:]]→ to match a character that is one of a class

Examples of classes that you will use

[: alnum:]→ from its name to match alpha – numeric characters

[:alpha:]→ To match your alpha characters

[:digit:]→ To **match numbers**

[:lower:]→ to match small letters

[:upper:]→ to match capital letters

Examples of Patterns

***→**All files

C*→ any file starts with c

h.txt* → any file starts with h and end with .txt

Data. [1-8][5-7][3-4] → any file starts with data and followed by these numbers

You can use the wildcards in GUI also, for example:

- Nautilus file manager (GNOME environment)

- Dolphin file manager (KDE environment)

Mkdir (this command is used to create directory)

[Youruser @ linux ~] $ mkdir directory

Also you can create more than one directory using the same line of command

[Youruser @ linux ~] $ mkdir d1 d2 d3 d4

cp (this command is used to copy directories and files)

[Youruser @ linux ~] $ cp d1 d2 d3

If you want to copy specific file from specific directory

30

[Youruser @ linux ~] $ cp f1 d1

mv (this command is used to move and rename directories and files)

[Youruser @ linux ~] $ mv d1

[Youruser @ linux ~] $ mv f1 d1

rm (this command is used to remove directories and files)

[Youruser @ linux ~] $ rm d1

• Be aware that if you are using the rm command on Linux, you cannot recover or undelete the file or the directory again!!!

ln (this command is used to create links)

To create hard link

[Youruser @ linux ~] $ ln f1 link

To create symbolic link

 [Youruser @ linux ~] $ ln -s f1 link

Hard links

31

It's the old way to create a link on original UNIX system, but it has some disadvantages

- cannot refer a file outside its system of files

- cannot refer to a directory

Symbolic links

It' the new or modern way to create a link on UNIX like system such as Linux , but this time without the disadvantages of the hard links, so now

- can refer a file outside its system of files

- can refer to a directory

Let' s practice some commands

[Youruser @ linux ~] $ cd

[Youruser @ linux ~] $ mkdir practice

Now we will create 2 directories inside the practice directory

[Youruser @ linux practice] $ mkdir d1 d2

Now it's time to copying ...

You will copy the passwd file from etc directory to the practice directory

[Youruser @ linux practice] $ cp /etc/passwd practice

Youruser @ linux :~/practice$ ls -l

total 12

drwxrwxr-x 2 Youruser Youruser 4096 Aug 1 06:20 d1

drwxrwxr-x 2 Youruser Youruser 4096 Aug 1 06:20 d2

-rw-r--r-- 1 Youruser Youruser 2195 Aug 1 06:25 practice

Now repeat the copying using verbose v

Youruser @ linux :~/practice$ cp -v /etc/passwd practice

'/etc/passwd' -> 'practice'

Youruser @ linux: ~/practice$ cp -i /etc/passwd practice

cp: overwrite 'practice'?

if you want to overwrite the file response with 'y', if not response with any other character like 'n'

now let's change the name of our file passwd to any other name

Youruser @ linux :~/practice$ mv passwd noname

Let's move it now

Youruser @ linux :~/practice$ mv noname d1

Then move it from d1 to d2

Youruser @ linux :~/practice$ mv d1/noname d2

Youruser @ linux :~/practice$ mv d2/noname

Then back it again

 Youruser @ linux :~/practice$ mv noname d1

Then we will move d1 into d2 and confirm with ls

Youruser @ linux :~/practice$ mv d1 d2

Youruser @ linux :~/practice$ ls –l d2

total 4
drwxrwxr-x 2 Youruser Youruser 4096 2008-01-11 06:06
dir1
Youruser @linux practice$ **ls -l d2/d1**
total 4
-rw-r--r-- 1 Youruser Youruser 1650 2017-01-8 16:33
noname

because d2 already existed , mv moved d1 into d2

let's back everything again

Youruser @ linux :~/practice$ mv d2/d1

Youruser @ linux :~/practice$ mv d1/noname

Hard Links Creating

Youruser @ linux :~/practice$ ln noname noname-hard

Youruser @ linux :~/practice$ ln noname d1/noname-hard

Youruser @ linux :~/practice$ ln noname d2/noname-hard

Let's take a look at our directory

Youruser @ linux :~/practice$ ls –l

drwxrwxr-x 2 Youruser Youruser 4096 2017-08-1 16:17 dir1

drwxrwxr-x 2 Youruser Youruser 4096 2017-08-1 16:17 dir2

-rw-r--r-- 4 Youruser Youruser 1650 2017-01-08-1 16:33 noname

-rw-r--r-- 4 Youruser Youruser 1650 2017-01-08-1 16:33 noname-hard

Let's add 'i' to the ls –l command and see

Youruser @ linux: ~/practice$ ls –li

total 16

12353539 drwxrwxr-x 2 Youruser Youruser 4096 2017-08-1 16:17 d1

12353540 drwxrwxr-x 2 Youruser Youruser 4096 2017-08-1 16:17 d2

12353538 -rw-r--r-- 4 Youruser Youruser 1650 2017-08-1 16:33 noname

12353538 -rw-r--r-- 4 Youruser Youruser 1650 2017-08-1 16:33 noname-hard

Symbolic Links Creating

Youruser @ linux: ~/practice$ ln -s noname noname-sym

Youruser @ linux: ~/practice$ ln -s ../noname d1/noname-sym

Youruser @ linux: ~/practice$ ln -s ../noname d2/noname-sym

Youruser @ linux: ~/practice$ ls –l d1

total 4

-rw-r--r-- 4 Youruser Youruser 1650 2017-08-1 16:33 noname-hard

lrwxrwxrwx 1 Youruser Youruser 6 2017-08-1 15:17 noname-sym -> ../noname

Youruser @ linux: ~/practice$ ln -s d1 d2-sym

Youruser @ linux: ~/practice$ ls –l

total 16

drwxrwxr-x 2 Youruser Youruser 4096 2017-08-1 15:17 d1

36

lrwxrwxrwx 1 Youruser Youruser 4 2017-08-1 14:45 dir1-sym -> d1

drwxrwxr-x 2 Youruser Youruser 4096 2017-08-1 15:17 d2

-rw-r--r-- 4 Youruser Youruser 1650 2017-08-1 16:33 noname

-rw-r--r-- 4 Youruser Youruser 1650 2017-08-1 16:33 noname-hard

lrwxrwxrwx 1 Youruser Youruser 3 2017-08-1 15:15 fun-sym -> noname

Files and directories removing

Youruser @ linux: ~/practice$ rm noname-hard

Youruser @ linux: ~/practice$ ls –l

total 12

drwxrwxr-x 2 Youruser Youruser 4096 2017-08-1 15:17 d1

lrwxrwxrwx 1 Youruser Youruser 4 2017-08-1 14:45 dir1-sym -> d1

drwxrwxr-x 2 Youruser Youruser 4096 2017-08-1 15:17 d2

-rw-r--r-- 3 Youruser Youruser 1650 2017-08-1 16:33 noname

Lrwxrwxrwx 1 Youruser Youruser 3 2017-08-1 15:15 noname-sym -> noname

Let i to our command

Youruser @ linux: ~/practice$ rm -i fun

rm: remove regular file `fun'? enter 'y' for yes or any other for no

Youruser @ linux: ~/practice$ ls -l

total 8

drwxrwxr-x 2 Youruser Youruser 4096 2017-08-1 15:17 d1

lrwxrwxrwx 1 Youruser Youruser 4 2017-08-1 14:45 dir1-sym -> d1

drwxrwxr-x 2 Youruser Youruser 4096 2017-08-1 15:17 d2

lrwxrwxrwx 1 Youruser Youruser 3 2017-08-1 15:15 noname-sym -> noname

Questions

1. What is the difference between hard and symbolic links?

2. Give an example of globbing or wildcards

3. Create 3 directories and put into them 3 files and remove all of the files

Chapter 4

Go deeper with the Command Line

What you will learn in this chapter

Φ Learn more commands

What you will need for this chapter

Φ PC with Linux / UNIX operating system

Let's try learn some new commands and see what will be happened

type command

Youruser @ linux:~$ type cd

cd is a shell builtin

Youruser @ linux:~$ type ls

ls is aliased to `ls --color=auto'

Youruser @ linux:~$ type less

less is /usr/bin/less

Youruser @ linux:~$ type mv

mv is /bin/mv

which command

Youruser @ linux:~$ which less

/usr/bin/less

Youruser @ linux:~$ which mv

/bin/mv

Youruser @ linux:~$ which ls

/bin/ls

Youruser @ linux:~$ which cp

/bin/cp

Help command

Youruser @ linux:~$ help cd

cd: cd [-L | [-P [-e]] [-@]] [dir]

Change the shell working directory.

Change the current directory to DIR. The default DIR is the value of the

HOME shell variable.

The variable CDPATH defines the search path for the directory containing

DIR. Alternative directory names in CDPATH are separated by a colon (:).

A null directory name is the same as the current directory. If DIR begins

with a slash (/), then CDPATH is not used.

If the directory is not found, and the shell option `cdable_vars' is set,

the word is assumed to be a variable name. If that variable has a value,

its value is used for DIR.

Options:

-L force symbolic links to be followed: resolve symbolic links in

DIR after processing instances of `..'

-P use the physical directory structure without following symbolic

links: resolve symbolic links in DIR before processing instances

of `..'

-e if the -P option is supplied, and the current working directory cannot be determined successfully, exit with a non-zero status

-@ on systems that support it, present a file with extended attributes

as a directory containing the file attributes

The default is to follow symbolic links, as if `-L' were specified.

`..' is processed by removing the immediately previous pathname component

back to a slash or the beginning of DIR.

Exit Status:

Returns 0 if the directory is changed, and if $PWD is set successfully when

-P is used; non-zero otherwise.

Another usage of the help command which is to describe the options of the command

Youruser @ linux:~$ mkdir --help

Usage: mkdir [OPTION]... DIRECTORY...

Create the DIRECTORY(ies), if they do not already exist.

Mandatory arguments to long options are mandatory for short options too.

-m, --mode=MODE   set file mode (as in chmod), not a=rwx - umask

  -p, --parents   no error if existing, make parent directories as needed

  -v, --verbose   print a message for each created directory

  -Z   set SELinux security context of each created directory

                    to the default type

    --context[=CTX] like -Z, or if CTX is specified then set the SELinux

                    or SMACK security context to CTX

    --help   display this help and exit

    --version output version information and exit

GNU coreutils online help: <http://www.gnu.org/software/coreutils/>

Full documentation at: <http://www.gnu.org/software/coreutils/mkdir>

or available locally via: info '(coreutils) mkdir invocation'

man command (to show the manual page)

Youruser @ linux:~$ man cp

CP(1)   User Commands
CP(1)

NAME

cp - copy files and directories

SYNOPSIS

cp [OPTION]... [-T] SOURCE DEST

cp [OPTION]... SOURCE... DIRECTORY

cp [OPTION]... -t DIRECTORY SOURCE...

DESCRIPTION

Copy SOURCE to DEST, or multiple SOURCE(s) to DIRECTORY.

Mandatory arguments to long options are mandatory for short options

too.

-a, --archive

same as -dR --preserve=all

--attributes-only

don't copy the file data, just the attributes

-b   like --backup but does not accept an argument

--copy-contents

copy contents of special files when recursive

-d   same as --no-dereference --preserve=links

-f, --force

       if an existing destination file cannot be opened, remove it and

       try again (this option is ignored when the -n option is also

       used)

-i, --interactive

       prompt before overwrite (overrides a previous -n option)

-H   follow command-line symbolic links in SOURCE

-l, --link

       hard link files instead of copying

-L, --dereference

Manual page cp(1) line 26 (press h for help or q to quit)

Info command

Youruser @ linux:~$ info ls

File: coreutils.info, Node: ls invocation, Next: dir invocation, Up: Directo\

ry listing

10.1 'ls': List directory contents

=====================================

The 'ls' program lists information about files (of any type, including

directories). Options and file arguments can be intermixed arbitrarily,

as usual.

For non-option command-line arguments that are directories, by

default 'ls' lists the contents of directories, not recursively, and

omitting files with names beginning with '.'. For other non-option

arguments, by default 'ls' lists just the file name. If no non-option argument is specified, 'ls' operates on the current directory, acting as

if it had been invoked with a single argument of '.'.

By default, the output is sorted alphabetically, according to the

locale settings in effect.(1) If standard output is a terminal, the

(some of the info you will get after typing the info command)

Alias (to create your commands)

Youruser @ linux:~$ type cd

cd is a shell builtin

Youruser @ linux:~$ type puty

bash: type: puty: not found

if you tried to write any name of command that is not built in the shell

you will get a message "bash: type: command: not found"

so let's create our command which is "puty"

Youruser @ linux:~$ alias puty='cd /usr; ls; cd -'

Now let's write the command

Youruser @ linux:~$ puty

bin games include lib local sbin share src x86_64-linux-gnu

/home/ Youruser

Youruser @ linux:~$ type puty

puty is aliased to `cd /usr; ls; cd -'

now let's delete the command or "using unalias"

Youruser @ linux:~$ unalias puty

Youruser @ linux:~$ puty

No command 'puty' found, did you mean:

Command 'putty' from package 'putty' (universe)

Questions

1. Describe the different types of commands

2. Create an alias using any name to do a specific function

3. Try the info and the man commands and explain the difference between them

Chapter 5

Searching

What you will learn in this chapter

Φ Text Searching

What you will need for this chapter

Φ PC with Linux / UNIX operating system

In this part you will learn how to search for a file using the command line

There are two commands you will need to find files on linux

● locate→ you can use this command to find files using their names

● find → This command can be used to find file in a directory hierarchy

Also these are commands help you to search and explore the files on linux

● xargs→ to help you in building command lines from the inputs

● touch → to change the time of your files

● stat → to show the file status

Let's do some hands-on work

Locate

Youruser @ linux:~$ locate bin/zip

/usr/bin/zip

/usr/bin/zipcloak

/usr/bin/zipdetails

/usr/bin/zipgrep

/usr/bin/zipinfo

/usr/bin/zipnote

/usr/bin/zipsplit

As you can see the locate program performs the search as a rapid database search , and then get you the outputs as substring , like if you want to search or find all programs that start with "zip" , so the ouput will be any pathname with zip such as the above output

You can combine the locate with grep to get more outputs

Youruser @ linux:~$ locate zip | grep bin

 /bin/bunzip2

/bin/bzip2

/bin/bzip2recover

/bin/gunzip

/bin/gzip

/usr/bin/funzip

/usr/bin/gpg-zip

/usr/bin/mzip

/usr/bin/preunzip

/usr/bin/prezip

/usr/bin/prezip-bin

/usr/bin/unzip

/usr/bin/unzipsfx

/usr/bin/zip

/usr/bin/zipcloak

/usr/bin/zipdetails

/usr/bin/zipgrep

/usr/bin/zipinfo

/usr/bin/zipnote

/usr/bin/zipsplit

/usr/lib/klibc/bin/gunzip

/usr/lib/klibc/bin/gzip

/usr/share/man/man1/prezip-bin.1.gz

Let's try the second command to find the files

Find

Youruser @ linux:~$ find ~

This will produce you a large list like the following

Let's count the number of files using wc

Youruser @ linux:~$ find ~ | wc –1

You will get 656

There are types of files that you will search for such as the following

● b → for the special device file type

● c → for the character device file

● d → for directories

● f → for the regular files

● l → for the symbolic links

Let's try an example

Youruser @ linux: ~$ find ~ -type f -name "*.JPG" -size +1M | wc -l

You will get the number of files of these preferences, if there are not such files you will get 0

In the previous line we used –name followed by the wildcard pattern

You can use these characters to find the files with specific sizes

- b→ for 512-byte block . the 512 byte is the default

- C→ for Bytes

- W→ for the 2-byte words

- K→ for kilobytes (one kilobyte = 1024 bytes)

- M→ for megabytes (one megabyte = 1048576 bytes)

- G → for gigabyte (one gigabyte = 1073741824)

The find command is supporting a very large number of tests

-cmin n → to match files that have been modified attributes (n for minutes)

-cnewer file → to match files that have been recently modified

-ctime n → to match files that have been modified in the last n*24 hours

-empty → to match any empty files

-group name→ to match any group of files using names or numbers

--iname pattern → such as the –name test

-inum n→ to match the files with n number

-mmin n→ to match files that have been modified in the last n minutes

-mtime → to match all files that have been modified in the last n*24 hours

-name pattern → to match all files with specific wildcards

-newer file → to match all files that have been modified recently

-nouser→ to match files that don't belong to any exist user

-nogroup → to match file that don't belong to any exist group

-perm mode→ to match all files that have set of permissions

-samefile name → to match all files that share any attribute like the file name

-size n → to match the files with size n

-type c → to match the files with type c

-user name → to match files that belong to any user name

Operators

If you even use all the above tests that find have, you will still need to use something called the logical operators (and, or, not…)

And → to match if both tests are true

Or → to match if one of the test is true

Not → to match if one is false

For example if you have two expressions

Experssion1	operator	Expression 2
True	-and	will be exceuted
False	-and	will not be exceuted
True	-or	will not be exceuted
False	-or	will be exceuted

Predefined Actions

The find command allows you to use some predefined actions like the following

-delete→ to delete the current file

-ls→ to perform action like the ls –dils command

-print→to show the output of the full pathname of the file

-quit → to quite if the match has been made

You can use print to delete files

Youruser @ linux: ~$ find ~ -type f -name '*.BAK' –delete

User Define Actions

You can also invoke commands that are arbitrary. You can do that with the –exec action, for example:

-exec your command {};

Youruser @ linux: ~$ find ~ -type f -name 'putty*' -ok ls -l '{}' ';'

< ls ... /home/ Youruser /bin/'putty > ? y

-rwxr-xr-x 1 Youruser Youruser 224 2017-08-02 12:53 /home/ Youruser /bin/'putty

< ls ... /home/ Youruser /'putty.txt > ? y

-rw-r--r-- 1 Youruser Youruser 0 2017-08-02 12:53 /home/me/'putty.txt

In the above example we used the string "putty" and execute the command ls , finally we used the –ok action to prompt the user before the ls command

Xargs

Youruser @ linux: ~$ find ~ -type f -name putty*' -print | xargs ls –l

-rwxr-xr-x 1 Youruser Youruser 224 2017-08-02 18:44 /home/ putty /bin/ putty

-rw-r--r-- 1 Youruser Youruser 0 2017-08-02 12:53 /home/ Youruser / putty.txt

The xargs command accepts the input and converts it into an argument

The find options

-depth: to process the file before the directory itself

-maxdepth levels: to set the max number of the levels

-mindepth levels: to set the min number of the levels

-mount: to traverse files that are mounted on other files

-noleaf: to scan DOS/windows file systems

Questions

1. List the file types that you will search for

2. What is the difference between the user defined actions and the pre-defined actions

3. Explain the usage of the following

- Xargs

- quit option

- the and operator

Chapter 6

Text processing

What you will learn in this chapter

Φ Text processing

What you will need for this chapter

Φ PC with Linux / UNIX operating system

Any UNIX like system such as the Linux operating system has a lot of text files for data storage, so there are a lot of tools to work with these data "text processing tools", mainly you will work with the programs that are used to text formatting

There are many types of Text

● Documents

● Web pages

● Email

● Source code

Now it's time to work with some commands

Cat

The cat command has many options to help you to visualize your text content. For example is the –A option that used to show non printing characters in your text, let's test this command

Youruser @ linux: ~$ cat > myfile.txt

Hello,

This is a file for testing, Thank you

Youruser @ linux: ~$ cat -A myfile.txt

Hello, $

This is a file for testing $

Thank you $

Let's try another option, which is the −ns

Youruser @ linux: ~$ cat > myfile.txt

This is

another option (-ns)

Youruser @ linux: ~$ cat -ns myfile.txt

   1   This is

   2

   3   another option (-ns)

Sort

The sort program/command is used to sort the contents of your input

It works like the cat command (the same technique)

Youruser @ linux: ~$ sort > myfile.txt

the first line

the second line

the third line

Youruser @ linux: ~$ cat myfile.txt

the first line

the second line

the third line

du

The du command is used to list the result of your summery in the pathname order

Youruser @ linux: ~$ du -s /usr/share/*

1580   /usr/share/2013.com.canonical.certification:checkb ox

16   /usr/share/2013.com.canonical.certification:plainbo x-resources

200   /usr/share/accounts

12   /usr/share/accountsservice

268   /usr/share/aclocal

8   /usr/share/acpi-support

20   /usr/share/activity-log-manager

8   /usr/share/adduser

432   /usr/share/adium

148	/usr/share/aisleriot
676	/usr/share/alsa
36	/usr/share/alsa-base
720	/usr/share/appdata
51280	/usr/share/app-install
12	/usr/share/application-registry
680	/usr/share/applications
856	/usr/share/apport
12	/usr/share/apps
8	/usr/share/apt
16	/usr/share/apturl
236	/usr/share/apt-xapian-index
7168	/usr/share/arduino
1624	/usr/share/aspell
16	/usr/share/avahi
19200	/usr/share/backgrounds
40	/usr/share/base-files
12	/usr/share/base-passwd
2256	/usr/share/bash-completion

12	/usr/share/binfmts
1156	/usr/share/branding
740	/usr/share/brasero
12	/usr/share/brltty
800	/usr/share/bug
12	/usr/share/build-essential
712	/usr/share/ca-certificates
12	/usr/share/ca-certificates-java
432	/usr/share/calendar
28	/usr/share/ccsm
236	/usr/share/checkbox-gui
12	/usr/share/click
7720	/usr/share/codeblocks
176	/usr/share/cogl
300	/usr/share/color
472	/usr/share/colord
12	/usr/share/columbus1
4228	/usr/share/command-not-found
208	/usr/share/common-licenses

1348	/usr/share/compiz
36	/usr/share/compizconfig
1428	/usr/share/consolefonts
52	/usr/share/console-setup
112	/usr/share/consoletrans
7448	/usr/share/cups
944	/usr/share/dbus-1
28	/usr/share/debconf
48	/usr/share/debhelper
8	/usr/share/debianutils
12	/usr/share/deja-dup
160	/usr/share/desktop-directories
436	/usr/share/dh-python
1396	/usr/share/dict
36	/usr/share/dictionaries-common
384	/usr/share/djvu
16	/usr/share/dns
8	/usr/share/dnsmasq-base
109440	/usr/share/doc

172	/usr/share/doc-base
40	/usr/share/dpkg
336	/usr/share/emacs
1328	/usr/share/empathy
8	/usr/share/enchant
148	/usr/share/eog
248	/usr/share/evince
12	/usr/share/evolution-data-server
5120	/usr/share/example-content
12	/usr/share/extra-xdg-menus
52	/usr/share/farstream
2892	/usr/share/file
8	/usr/share/file-roller
16	/usr/share/fontconfig
98596	/usr/share/fonts
6868	/usr/share/fonts-droid
16	/usr/share/foo2qpdl
1800	/usr/share/foo2zjs
68	/usr/share/gcc-4.9

956	/usr/share/gconf
184	/usr/share/GConf
28	/usr/share/gcr-3
440	/usr/share/gdb
28	/usr/share/gdm
428	/usr/share/gedit
8	/usr/share/geoclue-providers
4716	/usr/share/GeoIP
1432	/usr/share/gettext
4912	/usr/share/ghostscript
1976	/usr/share/glib-2.0
460	/usr/share/gnome
12	/usr/share/gnome-background-properties
36	/usr/share/gnome-bluetooth
32	/usr/share/gnome-control-center
1024	/usr/share/gnome-mahjongg
88	/usr/share/gnome-mines
32	/usr/share/gnome-online-accounts
32	/usr/share/gnome-session

28	/usr/share/gnome-shell
12	/usr/share/gnome-sudoku
32	/usr/share/gnome-user-share
140	/usr/share/gnome-video-effects
44	/usr/share/gnome-vpn-properties
16	/usr/share/gnupg
1612	/usr/share/groff
2504	/usr/share/grub
24	/usr/share/grub-gfxpayload-lists
96	/usr/share/gst-plugins-base
16	/usr/share/gstreamer-0.10
28	/usr/share/gstreamer-1.0
484	/usr/share/gtk-doc
68	/usr/share/gtk-engines
1584	/usr/share/gtksourceview-3.0
4148	/usr/share/guile
6084	/usr/share/gutenprint
116	/usr/share/gvfs
1244	/usr/share/hal

12	/usr/share/hardening-includes
90728	/usr/share/help
6864	/usr/share/help-langpack
13756	/usr/share/hplip
700	/usr/share/hunspell
60	/usr/share/hwdata
8872	/usr/share/i18n
412	/usr/share/ibus
1016	/usr/share/ibus-table
140524	/usr/share/icons
132	/usr/share/idl
180	/usr/share/im-config
24	/usr/share/indicator-application
20	/usr/share/indicators
1120	/usr/share/info
252	/usr/share/initramfs-tools
40	/usr/share/insserv
100	/usr/share/intltool-debian
12	/usr/share/iptables

748	/usr/share/java
1652	/usr/share/javazi
16	/usr/share/kde4
24	/usr/share/keyrings
88	/usr/share/language-selector
20	/usr/share/language-support
36	/usr/share/language-tools
8	/usr/share/libaudio2
8	/usr/share/libc-bin
676	/usr/share/libexttextcat
28	/usr/share/libgnomekbd
736	/usr/share/libgphoto2
1412	/usr/share/libgweather
1452	/usr/share/liblangtag
6300	/usr/share/liblouis
16	/usr/share/libnm-gtk
32	/usr/share/libparse-debianchangelog-perl
328	/usr/share/libquvi-scripts
27288	/usr/share/libreoffice

4	/usr/share/libsensors4
556	/usr/share/libthai
4192	/usr/share/libtimezonemap
116	/usr/share/libvisual-plugins-0.4
608	/usr/share/libwacom
28	/usr/share/lightdm
3580	/usr/share/lintian
12	/usr/share/linux-sound-base
29288	/usr/share/locale
10156	/usr/share/locale-langpack
12	/usr/share/locales
27404	/usr/share/man
12	/usr/share/man-db
108	/usr/share/maven-repo
1032	/usr/share/media-player-info
192	/usr/share/menu
12	/usr/share/metacity
5572	/usr/share/mime
36	/usr/share/mime-info

188	/usr/share/mimelnk
932	/usr/share/misc
332	/usr/share/mobile-broadband-provider-info
36	/usr/share/mousetweaks
12	/usr/share/mozilla
124	/usr/share/nano
20	/usr/share/nautilus-share
576	/usr/share/nm-applet
1992	/usr/share/notify-osd
888	/usr/share/nux
4	/usr/share/omf
20232	/usr/share/onboard
40	/usr/share/oneconf
80	/usr/share/open-vm-tools
240	/usr/share/orca
12	/usr/share/os-prober
16	/usr/share/p11-kit
4	/usr/share/package-data-downloads
44	/usr/share/pam

20	/usr/share/pam-configs
19396	/usr/share/perl
6396	/usr/share/perl5
484	/usr/share/pixmaps
96	/usr/share/pkgconfig
4	/usr/share/pkg-config-crosswrapper
12	/usr/share/plainbox-providers-1
24	/usr/share/pnm2ppa
828	/usr/share/polkit-1
12196	/usr/share/poppler
12	/usr/share/popularity-contest
260	/usr/share/ppd
20	/usr/share/ppp
244	/usr/share/pulseaudio
32	/usr/share/purple
296	/usr/share/python
188	/usr/share/python3
2640	/usr/share/python3-plainbox
168	/usr/share/python-apt

9952	/usr/share/qt4
9116	/usr/share/qt5
12	/usr/share/qtchooser
12	/usr/share/qtdeclarative5-ubuntu-web-plugin
8	/usr/share/readline
36	/usr/share/remmina
8	/usr/share/resolvconf
676	/usr/share/rhythmbox
8	/usr/share/rsyslog
352	/usr/share/samba
652	/usr/share/seahorse
64	/usr/share/session-migration
136	/usr/share/sgml
16	/usr/share/sgml-base
808	/usr/share/shotwell
88	/usr/share/simple-scan
696	/usr/share/snmp
3828	/usr/share/software-center
128	/usr/share/software-properties

13936	/usr/share/sounds
100	/usr/share/speech-dispatcher
33448	/usr/share/sphinx-voxforge-en
8	/usr/share/ssl-cert
1652	/usr/share/system-config-printer
12	/usr/share/systemd
8	/usr/share/sysv-rc
20	/usr/share/tabset
3632	/usr/share/tcltk
60	/usr/share/telepathy
3984	/usr/share/themes
16	/usr/share/thumbnailers
128	/usr/share/totem
828	/usr/share/transmission
64	/usr/share/ubuntu-drivers-common
172	/usr/share/ubuntu-release-upgrader
460	/usr/share/ufw
20	/usr/share/unattended-upgrades
1172	/usr/share/unity

1524	/usr/share/unity-control-center
120	/usr/share/unity-greeter
448	/usr/share/unity-scopes
44	/usr/share/unity-settings-daemon
56	/usr/share/unity-webapps
40	/usr/share/update-manager
104	/usr/share/update-notifier
220	/usr/share/upstart
12	/usr/share/url-dispatcher
76	/usr/share/usb-creator
20	/usr/share/usb_modeswitch
28	/usr/share/vim
40	/usr/share/vino
12	/usr/share/vte
1080	/usr/share/webbrowser-app
292	/usr/share/webkitgtk-3.0
5520	/usr/share/X11
108	/usr/share/xdiagnose
8	/usr/share/xgreeters

1660   /usr/share/xml

12   /usr/share/xml-core

8   /usr/share/xsessions

916   /usr/share/xul-ext

1816   /usr/share/yelp

To avoid showing this very long list you should write the following

Youruser @ linux: ~$ du -s /usr/share/* | head

1580   /usr/share/2013.com.canonical.certification:checkbox

16   /usr/share/2013.com.canonical.certification:plainbox-resources

200   /usr/share/accounts

12   /usr/share/accountsservice

268   /usr/share/aclocal

8   /usr/share/acpi-support

20   /usr/share/activity-log-manager

8   /usr/share/adduser

432   /usr/share/adium

148   /usr/share/aisleriot

We used head to limit the results

Youruser @ linux: ~$ du –s /usr/share/* | sort –nr | head

140524 /usr/share/icons

109440 /usr/share/doc

98596 /usr/share/fonts

90728 /usr/share/help

51280 /usr/share/app-install

33448 /usr/share/sphinx-voxforge-en

29288 /usr/share/locale

27404 /usr/share/man

27288 /usr/share/libreoffice

20232 /usr/share/onboard

In the above program we used the –nr option to get the reverse sort

We can use the ls command to sort the files by size

Youruser @ linux: ~$ ls -l /usr/bin | sort -nr -k 5 | head

-rwxr-xr-x 1 root root   6201336 Mar 21 2015 gdb

-rwxr-xr-x 1 root root   4324248 Jan 15 2015 shotwell

-rwxr-xr-x 1 root root   4091712 Mar 26 2015 python3.4m

-rwxr-xr-x 1 root root   4091712 Mar 26 2015 python3.4

-rwxr-xr-x 1 root root   3773512 Apr 2 2015 python2.7

-rwxr-xr-x 1 root root   3120496 Dec 9 2014 vim.tiny

-rwxr-xr-x 1 root root   2736624 Apr 10 2015 ld.gold

-rwxr-xr-x 1 root root   2540272 Apr 10 2015 dwp

-rwxr-xr-x 1 root root   2388960 Mar 19 2015 Xorg

-rwxr-xr-x 1 root root   1422328 Apr 16 2015 nautilus

Uniq

The uniq command is very similar to cat command but the uniq is a lightweight command / program

Youruser @ linux: ~$ uniq myfile.txt

the first line

the second line

the third line

Youruser @ linux: ~$ cat myfile.txt

the first line

the second line

the third line

There is no different between uniq and cat but the uniq removes the duplicate lines

Cut

The cut command / program is used to cut a line from a file and then output the line

Youruser @ linux: ~$ cut -f 3 myfile.txt

the first line

the second line

the third line

comm

You can use the comm program to compare between to text files and output the unique lines

Youruser @ linux: ~$ cat > file1.txt

r

t

y

k

l

Youruser @ linux: ~$ cat > file2.txt

r

t

n

m

l

q

Youruser @ linux: ~$ comm file1.txt file2.txt

      r

      t

   n

comm: file 2 is not in sorted order

   m

  l

  q

y

comm: file 1 is not in sorted order

k

l

diff

the diff command is very similar to the comm command which is used to detect any differences between files, but diff is more complex tool

and also the output will be in different style

Youruser @ linux: ~$ diff file1.txt file2.txt

3,4c3,4

85

< y

< k

> n

> m

5a6

> q

You can also use the –c option to the diff command as the following

Youruser @ linux: ~$ diff -c file1.txt file2.txt

*** file1.txt   2017-08-05 03:51:10.934914126 -0700

--- file2.txt   2017-08-05 03:51:40.610913457 -0700

****

*** 1,5 ****

  r

  t

! y

! k

l

--- 1,6 ----

r

t

! n

! m

l

+ q

Questions

1. Explain the types of files

2. What is the difference between the following commands?

- The diff and the comm commands

- The cat and the uniq commands

Chapter 7

Writing Scripts

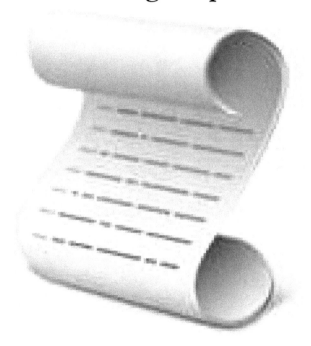

What you will learn in this chapter

Φ Writing Shell Scripts

Φ Understanding Shell Variables

What you will need for this chapter

Φ PC with Linux / UNIX operating system

Shell script is a file that has a set of instructions / commands.

The shell can read the file and execute the commands like the compiler or the interpreter

Steps to write your Shell Script

- write your script

- Make your script executable

- Save the script somewhere

Let's play

We will create the first shell script program

#!/bin/bash

This is your first script

echo ' Hello Shell Script '

This is a comment

The shell will ignore the comments; the comment is used to make your code more readable

If you want to run the script you should first write the path , if you don't you will get an error like this

Bash: hello_shell: command not found,

But you should write your command as the following command

Youruser @ linux: ~$./hello_Shell #the file name

Hello Shell!

You can view the content of The PATH using this command

Youruser @ linux: ~$ echo $PATH

/
home/me/bin:/usr/local/sbin:/usr/local/bin:/usr/sbin:/usr/bin:/sbin:

/bin:/usr/g

Let's create a project

Start with the HTML Code

```
<HTML>

<HEAD>

<TITLE> The Title</TITLE>

</HEAD>

<BODY>

Content

</BODY>

</HTML>
```

Save this as project.html (using any of text editors)

Then you can write the following script

```
#!/bin/bash

# Program to output a system information page

echo "<HTML>"

echo " <HEAD>"

echo " <TITLE>The Title</TITLE>"

echo " </HEAD>"

echo " <BODY>"
```

echo " Content."

echo " </BODY>"

echo "</HTML>"

now let's make it executable

Youruser @ linux: ~$ chmod 755 ~/bin/sys_info_page

Youruser @ linux: ~$ sys_info_page

Now you should see the HTML text on the screen, you will also view the text on your web browser

Youruser @ linux: ~$ sys_info_page > sys_info_page.html

Youruser @ linux: ~$ firefox sys_info_page.html

Let's make some changes on your program

Youruser @ linux: ~$ echo "<HTML>

> <HEAD>

> <TITLE>The Title</TITLE>

> </HEAD>

> <BODY>

> Page body.

> </BODY>

> </HTML>"

The second phase of your program (adding data)

```
#!/bin/bash

# Program show sys info

echo "<HTML>

<HEAD>

<TITLE>Sys Info Report</TITLE>

</HEAD>

<BODY>

<H1>Sys Info Report</H1>

</BODY>

</HTML>"
```

Variables

A variable is a stored area in the memory that holds your values

Let's add the variables to your program

```
#!/bin/bash

# Program to output a sys Info page

mytitle="Sys Info Report"

echo "<HTML>
```

```
<HEAD>

<TITLE>$mytitle</TITLE>

</HEAD>

<BODY>

<H1>$mytitle</H1>

</BODY>

</HTML>"
```

By creating the variable $mytitle and assign it to your value "Sys Info Report"

You can simply create a variable like the following example

[Youruser @ linux: ~$ var="ok"

Youruser @ linux: ~$ echo $var

ok

Youruser @ linux: ~$ echo $varl

Let's add some data to your program

```bash
#!/bin/bash

# Program to output a sys info page

myTITLE="Sys Info Report For $myHOSTNAME"

myCURRENT_TIME=$(date +"%x %r %Z")

TIMESTAMP="Generate $myCURRENT_TIME, by $myUSER"

echo "<HTML>

<HEAD>

<TITLE>$myTITLE</TITLE>

</HEAD>

<BODY>

<H1>$myTITLE</H1>

<P>$myTIMESTAMP</P>

</BODY>

</HTML>"
```

Shell functions

A function is a set of code or instruction can be called many times ("write one time and call it many times") , you can write the function in this way

Function name {

Instructions / commands

Return

}

Let's write your first function

#!/bin/bash

```
# Shell function myfunction

function myfunction {

echo "command 2"

return

}

# your program will start here

echo "command 1"
```

let's add some functions to your program

```bash
#!/bin/bash

# Program to output a sys info page

myTITLE="Sys Info Report For $myHOSTNAME"

CURRENT_TIME=$(date +"%x %r %Z")

myTIMESTAMP="Generate $myCURRENT_TIME, by
$myUSER"

myreport_uptime () {

return

}

myreport_disk_space () {

return

}

myreport_home_space () {

return

}

cat << _EOF_
```

```
<HTML>

<HEAD>

<TITLE>$myTITLE</TITLE>

</HEAD>

<BODY>

<H1>$myTITLE</H1>

<P>$myTIMESTAMP</P>

$(myreport_uptime)

$(myreport_disk_space)

$(myreport_home_space)

</BODY>

</HTML>

_EOF_
```

• You should keep in mind that your function must contain at least one command, and the return command is an optional

Variables types

● **Local variable:** you can use the local variable just inside the function body

● **Global variable:** the global variable is used inside and outside the **function body, here is an example**

```
#!/bin/bash

# local-myvars: script to show local variables

myfee=0 # myglobal variable foo

func () {

local foo # variable myfee local to func

myfee=1

echo "func: myfee = $myfee"

}

func_2 () {

local myfee # variable myfee local to func_2

myfee=2

echo "func_2: myfee = $myfee"

}
```

```
echo "global: myfee = $myfee"
```

func

let's echo the output

```
echo "global: myfee = $myfee"
```

func_2

```
echo "global: myfee = $myfee"
```

Youruser @ linux: ~$ local-myvars

global: myfee = 0

func: myfee = 1

global: myfee = 0

func_2: myfee = 2

global: myfee = 0

Youruser @ linux: ~$ sys_info_page

<HTML>

<HEAD>

<TITLE>System Info Report </TITLE>

</HEAD>

<BODY>

<H1>System Info Report For linux</H1>

100

```
<P>Generate 03/8/2017 04:02:10 PM EDT, by Youruser
</P>

</BODY>

</HTML>

myreport_uptime () {

echo "Func myreport_uptime executed."

return

}

myreport_disk_space () {

echo "Func myreport_disk_space executed."

return

}

myreport_home_space () {

echo "Func myreport_home_space executed."

return

}
```

And now you can run the script again

```
Youruser @ linux: ~$ sys_info_page

<HTML>
```

<HEAD>

<TITLE>System Information Report For linuxbox</TITLE>

</HEAD>

<BODY>

<H1>Sys Info Report H1>

<P>Generate 03/8/2017 05:17:26 AM EDT, by Youruser</P>

Func myreport_uptime executed.

Func myreport_disk_space executed.

Func myreport_home_space executed.

</BODY>

</HTML

Now you can see your three functions

● The first function

myreport_uptime () {

cat <<- _EOF_

<H2>mySystem myUptime</H2>

<PRE>$(myuptime)</PRE>

EOF

```
return

}
```

- The second function

```
myreport_disk_space () {

cat <<- _EOF_

<H2>myDisk Space Utilization</H2>

<PRE>$(df -h)</PRE>

_EOF_

return

}
```

- The third function

```
myreport_home_space () {

cat <<- _EOF_

<H2>myHome Space Utilization</H2>
```

```
<PRE>$(du -sh /home/*)</PRE>

_EOF_

return

}
```

Chapter 8

Looping and Flow Control

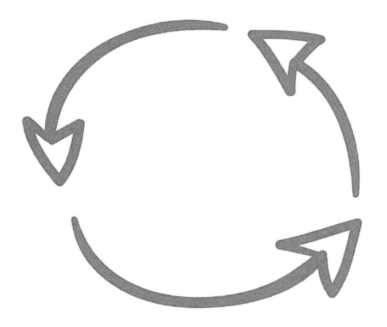

What you will learn in this chapter

Φ Understating loops using while / until

Φ Using delay and sleep functions

Φ Reading files with loops

Φ Working with shell variables

What you will need for this chapter

Φ PC with Linux / UNIX operating system

Flow control using IF

You can use if statement if you want to do something based on some conditions for example

If your age is more than 18 //this is the condition

You can drive a car with yourself //this is the action

If not //this is the condition

You can't drive a car //this is the action

This is called "logic"

Let's write the if in our shell

x=18

if [$x -eq 18]; then

echo "you can drive a car ."

else

echo "x you cannot drive a car ."

fi

Youruser @ linux: ~$ x=18

Youruser @ linux: ~$ if [$x -eq 18]; then echo " you can drive a car "; else echo

" you cannot drive a car "; fi

equals 15

Youruser @ linux: ~$ x=15

Youruser @ linux: ~$ if [$x -eq 15]; then echo " you cannot drive a car "; else echo

"you cannot drive a car "; fi

You cannot drive a car

Exit status

Your programs will give a value to your system when they will stop executing the instructions, this value from 0 to 255 , here is an example

Youruser @ linux: ~$ ls -d /usr/bin

/usr/bin

Youruser @ linux: ~$ echo $?

0[

Youruser @ linux: ~$ ls -d /bin/usr

ls: cannot access /bin/usr: No such file or directory

Youruser @ linux: ~$ echo $?

2

These two commands can be used to terminate (builtin commands)

Youruser @ linux: ~$ true

Youruser @ linux: ~$ echo $?

0

Youruser @ linux: ~$ false

Youruser @ linux: ~$ echo $?

1

You can also check the if command status using these commands

Youruser @ linux: ~$ if true; then echo "run unsuccessfully."; fi

run unsuccessfully

Youruser @ linux: ~$ if false; then echo "run successfully."; fi

Youruser @ linux: ~$

Test command

You will use this test command almost with the if statement, from its name it tests and compares many things

Take a Look at the following script

```
#!/bin/bash

# mytest-file: test and check the status of a file

myFILE=~/.bashrc

if [ -e "$myFILE" ]; then

if [ -f "$ myFILE " ]; then

echo "$ myFILE is a regular file."

fi

if [ -d "$ myFILE " ]; then

echo "$ myFILE is a directory."
```

```
fi

if [ -r "$ myFILE " ]; then

echo "$ myFILE is readable."

fi

if [ -w "$ myFILE " ]; then

echo "$ myFILE is writable."

fi

if [ -x "$ myFILE " ]; then

echo "$ myFILE is executable/searchable."

fi

else

echo "$ myFILE does not exist"

exit 1

fi

exit
```

here is some changes of the script

```
mytest_file () {

# test-file: Evaluate the status of a file
```

```
myFILE=~/.bashrc

if [ -e "$myFILE " ]; then

if [ -f "$myFILE " ]; then

echo "$myFILE is a regular file."

fi

if [ -d "$myFILE " ]; then

echo "$myFILE is a directory."

fi

if [ -r "$myFILE " ]; then

echo "$myFILE is readable."

fi

if [ -w "$myFILE " ]; then

echo "$myFILE is writable."

fi

if [ -x "$myFILE " ]; then

echo "$myFILE is executable/searchable."

fi

else

echo "$myFILE does not exist"
```

```
return 1

fi

}
```

Now let's work strings

```
#!/bin/bash

# mytest-string: test and check the value of a string

myANSWER=maybe

if [ -z "$myANSWER " ]; then

echo "please enter your answer." >&2

exit 1
```

```bash
fi

if [ "$myANSWER " = "yes" ]; then

echo "The answer is YES."

elif [ "$myANSWER " = "no" ]; then

echo "The answer is NO."

elif [ "$myANSWER " = "maybe" ]; then

echo "your answer is not accurate."

else

echo "your answer is invalid."

fi
```

Now it's time to show you some Integer Expressions

Here is the program

```bash
#!/bin/bash

# mytest-integer: evaluate the value of an integer.

myINT=-5

if [ -z "$myINT " ]; then
```

```
echo "your INT is empty." >&2

exit 1

fi

if [ $ myINT -eq 0 ]; then

echo "your INT is zero."

else

if [ $myINT -lt 0 ]; then

echo "your INT is negative."

else

echo "your INT is positive."

fi

if [ $(( myINT % 2)) -eq 0 ]; then

echo " your INT is even."

else

echo "your INT is odd."

fi

fi
```

In the following script you will get the new version of the test

```bash
#!/bin/bash

# mytest-integer2: test and check the value of an integer.

myINT=-5

if [[ "$ myINT " =~ ^-?[0-9]+$ ]]; then

if [ $ myINT -eq 0 ]; then

echo " your INT is zero."

else

if [ $ myINT -lt 0 ]; then

echo "your INT is negative."

else

echo "your INT is positive."

fi

if [ $(( myINT % 2)) -eq 0 ]; then

echo " your INT is even."

else

echo "your INT is odd."

fi
```

```bash
fi

else

echo "your INT is not an integer." >&2

exit 1

fi
```

Also you can write the above script in much simple way like this

```bash
#!/bin/bash

# mytest-integer2a: test and check the value of an integer.

myINT=-5

if [[ "$ myINT " =~ ^-?[0-9]+$ ]]; then

if ((myINT == 0)); then

echo "your INT is zero."

else

if ((myINT < 0)); then

echo "your INT is negative."

else

echo "your INT is positive."
```

```
fi

if (( (((myINT % 2)) == 0)); then

echo "your INT is even."

else

echo "your INT is odd."

fi

fi

else

echo "your INT is not an integer." >&2

exit 1

fi
```

Let's combine expressions using the logical operators

```bash
#!/bin/bash

# mytest-integer3: determine if an integer is within a

# specified range of values.

myMIN_VAL=1

myMAX_VAL=100

myINT=50

if [[ "$myINT " =~ ^-?[0-9]+$ ]]; then

if [[myINT -ge myMIN_VAL && myINT -le
myMAX_VAL ]]; then

echo "$myINT is within $myMIN_VAL to
$myMAX_VAL."

else

echo "$myINT is out of range."

fi

else

echo "your INT is not an integer." >&2

exit 1

fi
```

Here is another example

```bash
#!/bin/bash

# mytest-integer4: determine if an integer is outside a

myMIN_VAL=1

myMAX_VAL=100

myINT=50

if [[ "$myINT" =~ ^-?[0-9]+$ ]]; then

if [[ ! (myINT -ge myMIN_VAL && myINT -le
myMAX_VAL) ]]; then

echo "$myINT is outside $myMIN_VAL to
$myMAX_VAL."

else

echo "$myINT is in range."

fi

else

echo "your INT is not an integer." >&2

exit 1
```

fi

Looping

Looping is a repeated execution of instructions based on some conditions

While loops

You can construct a loop using while statement

Example :

#!/bin/bash

#while-counting: show a the number series

Count = 0

While[[$count –le 5]]; do

echo $count

count = $((count +1))

done

echo "done"

This is the output of the script

While-count

0

1

2

3

4

Done

Let's explain you the while loop

While commands; do commands; done

Like the if while evaluates exit status of a group of commands

If the exit status is zero, so the program will execute the instruction inside your loop , like the above program It started from 0 unit it reached to 4 and get out from the loop

We can create a menu using the loop

#!/bin/bash

while-menu: a menu program

DELAY=5 # 5 seconds to display the results

while [[$Response != 0]]; do

```
clear

cat <<- _END_

Please Select:

1. Show Info

2. Show your Space

3. Show your Utilization

0. Exit

_END_

read -p "Enter your choice [0-3] > "

if [[ $ Response =~ ^[0-3]$ ]]; then

if [[ $ Response == 1 ]]; then

echo "Your Hostname: $HOSTNAME"

uptime

sleep $DELAY

fi

if [[ $ Response == 2 ]]; then

df -h

sleep $DELAY

fi
```

```
if [[ $ Response == 3 ]]; then

if [[ $(id -u) -eq 0 ]]; then

echo "Home Space Utilization (All Users)"

du -sh /home/*

else

echo " Utilization ($USER)"

du -sh $HOME

fi

sleep $DELAY

fi

else

echo "Invalid choice."

sleep $DELAY

fi

done

echo "exit."
```

Get out from the loop

Bash has builtin commands that can be used to control your flow inside the loop (break and continue). The break command terminates the loop and the program will go to execute the next statement. The continue

Command also is used to skip the rest of the loop

Let's use the **break** and **continue** in our script

#!/bin/bash

while-menu2: a menu program

DELAY=5 # Number of seconds to show results

while true; do

clear

cat <<- _END_

Please Select:

1. Show Info

2. Show your Space

3. Show your Utilization

0. Exit

END

read -p "Enter your choice [0-3] > "

if [[$ Response =~ ^[0-3]$]]; then

if [[$ Response == 1]]; then

```
echo "your Hostname: $HOSTNAME"

uptime

sleep $DELAY

continue

fi

if [[ $ Response == 2 ]]; then

df -h

sleep $DELAY

continue

fi

if [[ $ Response == 3 ]]; then

if [[ $(id -u) -eq 0 ]]; then

echo " Utilization (All Users)"

du -sh /home/*

else

  echo " Utilization ($USER)"

du -sh $HOME

fi

sleep $DELAY
```

```
continue

fi

if [[ $ Response == 0 ]]; then

break

fi

else

echo "Invalid choice."

sleep $DELAY

fi

done

echo "exit."
```

In the above script we used endless loop (**while true**) that means it will loop forever, the loop will never end

Until

The until command is like the while but you can use in different way

Instead of exiting a loop when the status is not zero, it does the opposite

```
#!/bin/bash

# until-count: show the number series

count=0

until [[ $count -gt 7 ]]; do

echo $count

count=$((count + 1))

done

echo "done".
```

Reading files

```
#!/bin/bash

# while-read: read lines from a file

while read Distribution version release; do

printf "Distributions: %s\tVersion: %s\tReleased: %s\n" \

$ distribution \
```

$ver \

$re

done

done < Distributions.txt

You can redirect the file to the loop by writing the following

#!/bin/bash

while-read2: read lines from a file

sort -k 1,1 -k 2n Distributions.txt | while read Distribution version release; do

printf " Distribution: %s\tVersion: %s\tReleased: %s\n" \

$ distribution \

$ver \

$re

Done

Questions

1. What is the usage of (delay and sleep) functions?

2. Write a script to show numbers from 3 to 11 using while command

3. Write the example 2 but this time using the **until** command

Chapter 9

Troubleshooting and Debugging

What you will learn in this chapter

Φ Learn how to debug your scripts

What you will need for this chapter

Φ PC with Linux / UNIX operating system

Your script not always will be simple, but more complex, so you should take a look at what will happen if something go wrong, in this part you will learn the different types of errors

Syntactic Errors

#!/bin/bash

trouble: script to explain errors

num=3

if [$num = 3]; then

echo "your Number is equal to 3."

else

echo "Number is not equal to 3."

Fi

Youruser @ linux: ~$ trouble

Number is equal to 3.

The script run successfully

If we change something in our script

#!/bin/bash

trouble: script to show errors

number=3

if [$number = 3]; then

echo "your Number is equal to3.

else

echo "your Number is not equal to 3."

fi

You will get the following

Youruser @ linux: ~$ trouble

/home/ Youruser /bin/trouble: line 10: unexpected EOF while looking for matching `"'

/home/ Youruser /bin/trouble: line 13: syntax error: unexpected end of file

- There are two errors in our script, the closing quote and the syntax of if command

Unexpected Tokens

This is another common mistake is to forget to complete a command like the if or while

#!/bin/bash

trouble: script to explain errors

number=3

if [$number = 3] then

echo " your Number is equal to 3"

else

echo " your Number is not equal to 3."

fi

You will get the following

Youruser @ linux: ~$ trouble

/home/ Youruser /bin/trouble: line 9: syntax error near unexpected token

`else'

/home/ Youruser /bin/trouble: line 9: `else'

It's very possible to have errors that occur in a script. Maybe the script will be executed fine and other times it will be failed the reason of that is something called an expansion

```
#!/bin/bash

# trouble: script to show  errors

Number=3

if [ $number= 3 ]; then

echo "Your Number is equal to 3."

else

echo "Your Number is not equal to 3."

fi
```

Youruser @ linux: ~$ trouble

/home/ Youruser /bin/trouble: line 7: [: =: unary operator expected

Number is not equal to 3

Logic Errors

Logic errors is the second type of errors that you will find, the interpreter can't catch the logic errors

There are also common types of errors

• Incorrect conditional commands like if/else/ then

• the off by on errors , this kind of errors can be occurred when you code loops with counters

Debugging

After testing and finding errors in your script, the next step will be to fix these errors, this process is called "debugging"

Let's take a look at the next script

if [[-d $dir_myname]]; then

if cd $dir_myname; then

rm *

else

echo "cannot change directory to '$dir_myname'" >&2

exit 1

fi

else

echo "there is no directory: '$dir_myname'" >&2

exit 1

fi

echo " now we are deleting files" >&2

```
if [[ -d $dir_myname ]]; then

if cd $dir_myname; then

echo "we are deleting files" >&2

rm *

else

echo "cannot change directory  to '$dir_myname'" >&2

exit 1

fi

else

echo "there is no  directory: '$dir_myname'" >&2

exit 1

fi

echo " complete" >&2

delete-script

preparing to delete files

deleting files

deletion complete

Youruser @ linux: ~$

if [ $number = 3 ]; then
```

```
echo "Your Number is equal to 3."

else

echo "Your Number is not equal to 3."

Fi
```

Questions

1. **List the types of errors**

2. **What is debugging?**